RHYMES

By

John Paul Bernett

*To Clive
Thanks mate!
JPBernett*

© Copyright John Paul Bernett
 All rights reserved. No part of this book may be reproduced, stored, or transmitted by any means—whether auditory, graphic, mechanical, or electronic—without written permission of both publisher and author, except in the case of brief excerpts used in critical articles and reviews. Unauthorized reproduction of any part of this work is illegal and is punishable by law.
Published by Dark One Publishing Limited
ISBN: 978-0-9926173-6-3

Printed by Book Printing UK
Remus House, Coltsfoot Drive, Peterborough, PE2 9BF

Forward

This is a selection of poetry that I write whilst working on my novels. I don't know why they come into my head, they just do. I have decided to put them all into one place, and this is it – the aptly named RHYMES…for I don't pretend to be a poet, and I shouldn't really be a writer, but for some strange reason I am – so, rather than just cast these rhymes aside, I thought for my own amusement I would put them in this folder…

….and then somebody asked me to share

BELIEF

I am writing a book, I told some friends –
a proper story, from beginning to end.
I will be an author – you know, like Jules Verne –
they said, "The way you spell, you'll crash and burn!"
Not dejected was I, because I already knew –
my script was half done, they hadn't a clue!
My sights were set…I would aim high!
This isn't a dream, no pie in the sky!
They knew of my dyslexia and dismissed me, laughing –
my musings to them only fit for the trash-bin.
So I carried on typing my story –
not for elation, nor for glory…
But to show the world what my dad said was true!
"If you want to do it son, it's all up to you!"
And I carried on through chapter after chapter –
for me it was hard, but that did not matter…
Dyslexia is a word, not a rule of life!
No longer will I hide or let it give me strife.
Because my book is now finished! Published and true!
Please don't let dyslexia ever stop YOU.

THE JOURNEY

The sunshine long, the nighttime short –
as we begin our last great journey,
To leave behind what we knew –
the worry, the want, being lonely.
I care not of things of a bygone age –
I care not of possessions nor of wage…
I pay no mind to the waning life,
for life had no care for me…
For here we are, alone on a boat –
nothing about us but sea.
Oh such a life now this is!
To wander wherever we please –
To catch the tide and sail out onto life's ebbing seas.

YOUNG LOVE

As I look from my chair and watch the world go by,
I can see you both through my mind's eye…
Oh the joy of being fit and young!
With a song of love about to be sung…
The strolls, holding hands, plans to be planned,
Sitting there until it's dark.
That one last kiss made you miss the bus,
 then running home in such a rush.
As I sit here, I still live these things,
and bask in the joy that true love brings…
But to all of you with fire in your heart –
enjoy this time, for it's only the start.

THE GATHERING

Fire glow in the dead of night –
my friends and I gather, to great delight…
With athame in hand, wand and candle,
you would find it hard to handle…
The Sun and the Moon are bright, and true –
Just objects in the sky to someone like you…
For I am a witch, I'm different to you –
you can tell by my words, the things that I do…
My Gods and Goddesses are kind and loving…
Your Gods are fearsome, warlike, and forboding…
Every war that has ever been fought
can be traced back to religious thought.
Come, take my hand, and you will see –
how beautiful we all could be,
Yet you won't listen, and our planet will burn –
When will mankind ever learn?

FRIEND

A friend is a friend – will you be a friend to me?

Will you take me on, and help me see?

Can you lift my heart and make it sing?

Happiness for me…will you bring?

To this new friendship, what do I have to offer…

Love and more love, forever after!

For I am lost and need to be found…

Taken inside to be safe, and sound.

Will you walk on by, or be my friend?

I would be loyal to the end…

Oh please stop, and show me some pity!

I'm just a poor, lost little kitty.

THE REAPER AND I

The Reaper reaps and I dig the hole –
I prepare your space, he reaps your soul.
Upon your life his scythe will fall –
Then I will get your fatal call.
Just little old me, and my trusty spade
Will dig the hole to make your grave.
This life you have is but three score years and ten –
So get all of your living and loving done by then.
It makes no difference to Him be you judge, nurse or pauper,
He will despatch you to your hereafter.
His icy breath upon your neck you will feel –
As he snaps your seventh seal.
Then this life will ebb, but you'll go on –
So the next life beckons…which one have you won?
The good life of ease which some call 'Heaven'…
Or a hard life of doom in some dark cavern?
A cavern of the mind for your past deeds…
Or a walk in the park with everything you need?
And again, live, you will – for die again, you must…
And into the Reaper's realm again you put your trust.
Then you meet me again, with my trusty spade –
When into the ground again you are laid.

PEOPLE WHO JUDGE

As I walk and slowly pass you by,

I see that look within your eye -

In some strange way you seem disgusted –

but my clothes are new! Not soiled, or dusted…

You pay that no mind, as your expression clearly shows –

carry on bimbo, in your slapdash clothes!

For your fashion will change in the blink of an eye…

my clothes have history that won't pass me by.

So remember the very next time you scowl at a Goth –

We are not slaves to fashion! And you can FUCK OFF.

BOUND SOULS

Can it be that you are mine?

Will you stay with me till the end of time?

Through this life and all those to come –

Just to be my special one.

To follow our path that is everlasting –

From when we tied the knot to our Eternal Handfasting.

Our lives to come may still be hard to live –

But all of my efforts you know I will give.

Tears from you may still be cried –

But with me at your side, we shall abide…

And that's where I shall be forever more…

For you're the one that I adore.

And in my twilight hours, when you I must leave –

You will meet me again…you just have to believe.

PAST LIVES

Do I know you? Have we met before?

In another life perhaps by a distant shore?

That glance you gave was so familiar to me…

The way you walk, how you talk – could you be?

For I have wandered far and wide…

I've sat on the harbour on every ebb tide.

To see your face,

To feel your embrace.

Do I know you? Let me guess your name…

Can it really be you? Or am I insane?

It is you! Your presence I feel…

Come see me now! To you I appeal.

Do you know me? Please search your feelings…

Come find me now…my heart is bleeding!

She walks my way with a question in her eye…

She stops…not passing me by!

'Do I know you?' I hear her ask…

I think you do…from your distant past.

MY HERO

I remember sitting upon my dad's knee –
I remember the stories he would tell me.
Of monsters, and spacemen, and cowboys out West…
These were the stories that I loved best.
His descriptive ways, his wonderful tone
Made him the best storyteller I have ever known.
But now, I am he, and you are me –
I am the storyteller he used to be…
And I thank my dad for so many things…
But storytelling is one that such happiness brings.
My dad was my hero – so strong, so true –
In my eyes there was nothing that he couldn't do.

FRIENDS

I took my wife out to lunch

To our favourite place with the usual bunch.

The friends who know us and make us feel good –

To go anywhere else we never would!

A greeting, a smile, a lovely warm welcome…

In this day and age you'll find it seldom!

And where would you find a place such as this?

Where the food is excellent, whatever the dish?

In London? Paris? Milan or New York?

No, my friends, you'll find it in Scunthorpe!

And we had our lunch, just one of many –

At the wonderfully friendly Frankie & Benny's.

CHILDHOOD MEMORIES

As a boy I wanted to be an actor upon the stage –
Or standing tall against a villain's rage…
A spaceman wearing a silver suit!
Or a deep-sea diver with those big lead boots…
I wanted to be a cowboy, and cut them off at the pass –
And chase Indians across the prairie through that long, tall grass.
With a colander on my head I would drive my tank!
Or ride with Jessie James as we robbed a bank…
I would fly a Spitfire and loop-de-loop –
Or play football with my favourite group…
I was the Lone Ranger and my dog was Tonto –
Or Billy the Kid on his bucking bronco!
My draw was the fastest in the West –
There wasn't a gunslinger I couldn't best!
I had no need of a Playstation, X-Box or computer –
My imagination made me the finest sharpshooter…
And when at the end of the day I ran out of steam –
I lived it all again as I laid down to dream.

A RALEIGH CHOPPER

'Can I have a Raleigh Chopper for Christmas, Mam?'

I asked in '72.

'You will have to ask your dad,' she said, 'We can't afford one new!'

'It's the latest bike, Mam, it won't cost a lot!'

At 32 pounds, my dad asked me, 'Do you think you're on your father's yacht?'

'But it's great dad! It has a big back wheel! And a small one on the front! And a long black seat with ape-hanger bars…it's really what I want!'

'Oh yes!' said he, 'I know someone selling one of these…'

'Please buy it dad!' I pleaded, as I fell down to my knees.

All through December I waited for my prize…

And when I finally saw the thing I could not believe my eyes!

It had a small wheel at the front, and a big one at the back…

But the style and grace of the one I wanted, this one sadly lacked.

The main thing I didn't like – and I had to be quite blunt…

Was the sit-up-and-beg handlebars and the basket at the front…

'This is not a chopper!' I said, and 'This I do not like!'

'I've seen this before!' I said, 'It's Eric Killbourne's Butcher-Shop bike!'

'But not anymore!' Said he, 'It now belongs to you –

Fix it up a bit and do not be so blue!

And YOU can make it special! The bike that only YOU will own –

And do you know what he said was true!

I kept that bike until I was fully grown.

A VAMPYRIC KISS

To the dead-still night my unbeating heart calls…
And a tall, dark stranger whose drug I need when nighttime falls.
A kiss so deep it drains body and soul –
Either of which I would gladly give my all…
To this Gothic Entity that I call my friend –
Who found me lain in bed at my life's end…
And now forever undead, my love for Him does grow –
I wear the scars of love upon my neck that I do proudly show.
The fearful sight of my gaunt, pale complexion…
A deathly beautiful face that casts no reflection –
Will haunt you forever even though you prayed…
From my old life of drudgery I could not be saved.
But this dark life of blood-lust he lavished upon me…
In that dark ruined Abbey by the North Sea –
Was started with love and the reassurance of bliss…
Given to me by that Vampyric kiss.

HAVE A CARE

I look about me and see people going about their everyday life –
Young and old – some are happy, some are sad, some full of strife.
I look at their faces, their smiles, their eyes…
And wonder of their souls….that eyes can't hide.
Some seem restless, others calm, as they walk by me arm in arm –
They do not see me they just walk on by –
They don't hear my plea, nor see me cry.
They are all too busy with their important lives…
Finding new backs to place their knives…
The rat race has left me sat here in my rags –
Walk on by with your Armani bags…
Fifty pence – that's all – help me, please?
Life has brought me to my knees.
I am not a criminal, lazy or hopeless…
I'm one of thousands like me…just destitute, and homeless.

LOVE

Love is a priceless treasure to behold –
It changes you, be you young, or old...
To lay on a beach and hear water lap the sand –
Being there with your lover hand in hand.
A kiss in the moonlight as the sand grows cold –
Two beating hearts as you become bold...
The rhythm of the sea as it lavishes the shore –
The taste of pleasure, of our Amour...
As your fingers into the sand deep grooves do make –
You know her desires are yours to take.
Two naked bodies, proud and free –
There for the whole wide world to see;
For their love is real – not empty, nor fake –
Love is everlasting for two people to make.
Man and Woman, Woman and Woman, Man and Man –
It matters not, my friends – get it how you can...
For love is glorious...and it will happen to you –
Just love each other no matter what you do. <3

HATE

Hate is such a waste of time, it brings you nothing but pain –

It gives you much to lose, and nothing at all to gain.

To hate someone and not know why, to ignore them and pass them by;

Is being childish and immature – not to mention dumb and insecure.

But to bite your lip and ask them why…you would be surprised by their reply –

And then make up and just be friends…if this could just become the trend!

We would have more love and much less hate –

This can happen – it's not too late!

So please, don't hate someone just because they are different –

They may be a person of some great significance!

To live without hate just breeds love – then you would find love & peace go

Hand in Glove. ☐

A BETTER WAY

Some people try to live their lives the best way that they can –

Others try to get through theirs working to a plan.

A lot of people barge through this life with no care for mankind;

And most of us who do care are unfortunately left behind.

Because the powers that be push us aside, and bad this makes us feel –

They do not care as they charge through, hoping we will kneel.

We are governed by millionaire business-people whose profits must be met –

With more & more taxation on ordinary people, you can bet!

For they won't tax the rich as much – because the rich are they…

It's time it wasn't they who governed…there must be a better way.

It's just an idea to get real people who understand life, and its needs –

And not some old-school-tie business-person with portfolios and deeds.

TO BEV FROM MOM

People stare and are often rude, some of them nasty, straightforward and crude.

It seems my weight is difficult for them to take – as if my life isn't bad enough, for God's sake!

But you won't hear me hit back at you…for I am polite…it's not what I do.

My world is my daughter, who cares for me…

Through her, I get out – and I see what she sees!

I hear through her ears, she tells me what's new –

She shows me things that I never knew!

My life isn't pointless…like some people think…

With her stories from England, I'm tickled pink!

I now finally get to see England's green and pleasant land –

It's just as if I am holding her by the hand –

So if you think my life has no glee…

I'm sorry to inform you – you're not looking at me…

For through her eyes, I fly like a bird…

And hear through her ears! You might think it absurd!

Although I'm confined to my chair with disability –

I live my daughter's life vicariously. <3

DEATH

Bright light before me – a fiery pit behind…
Which will be the one set by for me to find?
What direction do I take…can I be the one to decide?
The brightness is too great for me to reside…
But the fire is the pit of everlasting damnation…
The other is supposed to be my lasting salvation –
Is the choice really mine? Let's try and see –
I'm not sure if either one is right for me…
So I walk towards the bright light – here I come…
The next thing is a scream as a Doctor slaps my bum!
I'm born again! Or so it seems….to a brand new life!
And as I could walk towards the light it won't be full of strife!
But what if the pit was my end…what would be my path?
To live a life of torture and feel the Devil's wrath?
But is that Biblical 'mumbo jumbo' taught to keep us in fear?
It's just the thing a young impressionable doesn't want to hear…
But I have found the way of life is much simpler to be –
You will find to live your life is just like being a tree…
In Spring you're born and the sap does rise and leaves begin growing –
Then all through the Summertime the sap does slow its flowing –
When Autumn comes, the end is near as your leaves begin to fall –
When Winter comes, the tree is dead – it has no life at all!
Then Springtime arrives again! The tree begins to grow!
Just as you will do, like a sapling, popping out from the snow…
So see, my friends? Death is not as frightening as you thought…
It's not at all how we all thought – It's just how we were taught.

BIG SPORTSMAN

Today I watched a bird flying in the sky –
It was strange how that bird was attracted to my eye…
Majestically soaring, beautifully-winged thing –
To me, much enjoyment it really did bring.
I watched it rise to the heavens – free to soar –
I heard a loud bang…and then it was no more.
A beautiful pheasant, so young and free –
Was now to be some posh twat's tea.
A 'sport' they say – but I say nay –
Why make birds your lawful prey?
When a clay pigeon would serve you with no death…
But it's that very thing that catches your breath…
And gives you a 'high'…you are a big man –
You showed that little bird just how you can
Aim and shoot while it's on the rise –
What a worthless shit you are – you so many despise.

PATHS

In life we have many different paths to take –

Some we take for ourselves, some for others' sake.

If looking in a mirror, reflecting your life's track –

You might be surprised at what you see when you look back.

If the path you chose for yourself is overgrown, and hard to see at all…

But the path you chose for others is there, then you have walked tall.

For to help yourself and to cut off all others,

Is a selfish life and unfulfilled without friends, sisters or brothers.

Sisters and brothers are not always your family members –

But can be friends you made whose love is equally as tender…

Blood is thicker than water, they say – well mine must be full of Warfarin;

Because some of my family cut me off with hurtful things and squabbling.

I don't let that change my path because I still like to lend a hand –

My paths are many, and not overgrown, and have made grooves in the sand.

I'm a happy man with few regrets and a lot to be thankful for…

A loving wife, some great kids, who I'll protect forever more.

The sword at my side is for casting circles, my pen is a release –

I have no need of hate or war, I just long for peace.

Some say the pen can be mightier than the sword –

Well I have both – so I will never be bored.

So while you go through your life look back one day and see –

Long straight paths with friends on them all waving back at thee…

For how sad would it be when you look back and find there's only one –

When your paths could have been many if the right things you had done.

LIFE

Tonight I saw a shooting star blaze across the sky...
And in a way that is how my life has passed me by –
Today I wished my eldest son a happy 33rd birthday...
It seems he was newborn and in my arms only yesterday.
Hunter came along when he was only 8 –
And now he is 16 and he is out on his first date.
A lot of people, I have lost, their memories never fade –
The fun I've had, the laughter, the friends that I have made.
I never seem to grow up, and for that I am glad –
Playing on the pit hills, the fun that I have had –
I no longer think of darker times, although they do exist...
I never long for the things I might have one time missed.
For here I am, a happy man with the one that I adore;
And here I'll be by her side, now and forever more.

BY YOUR SIDE

I draw my sword across my hand, the blood I spill for you –
I am here through your always and everything you do;
Your highs and lows, doubts and fears, your happiness and love –
At your flanks, front and back – even from above.
Protecting you – loving you – just being here...
So be still, my special one, for you have none to fear.
Your path has been long, filled with pain and hard for you to take –
All your deeds before we met were for your son and mother's sakes;
Your mother is now safe, your son is grown, so now it's time for you –
To put the past behind you and look forward to your life anew.
The past is bleak and hurtful, your future though, is bright –
All the bad times are now gone, swirling out of sight.
The things you have accomplished since landing on our shore
Are manifold – you were Wednesday, in our own store...
And loved by many, all of whom are wishing you be well –
So lift that chin and face your future – the rest can go to Hell.
And fight you will – for I know you, your strength is there for all to see;
Who else could have worn your shoes and as strong as you, be?
So here we go, one last push and your life again will flow –
And amongst your friends you will walk again with your special glow.
When that day comes, my sword back in its scabbard will be –
And I will resume my place, just one step behind thee.
Then you will be free to live again and life your head up high –
Because I am with you, sword in hand, until the day I die.

AND SO TO BED

A swirling mist, tired eyes, and again I fall asleep;
In your arms, on your bed, all my secrets you do keep –
The last thing I see at night and the first thing at my awakening
Is your beautiful face in the moonlight, and when the dawn is breaking.
To stroke your face and kiss your lips as your eyes begin to open
Is all I need to make my day before a word is spoken.

MOTHER

If I was to fall and hurt my knee,
I knew you'd always be there for me –
If I had bad dreams that made me cry,
You would chase them all away, bye-bye;
Through all my troubles and my doubt
You would always sort them out.
For my mum was Wonder Woman, though she didn't have a cape;
Everything she did was for someone else's sake.
She sent me off to school every day –
And whispered encouragement in her own sweet way;
She taught me things no teacher would know –
When to hide my feelings, when to let them show.
But most of all she taught me how to love,
In the right direction her gentle shove –
And now I'm a man and she is an angel;
I can look at her photo and I am able
To bring back her smile, her looks and her grace –
So once again, I can see her face. <3

THE FOUR HORSEMEN

The Storm Clouds of War chase away the blue –

The sound of sixteen hooves galloping to you –

Upon four horses the Riders draw close,

To deliver their package that Congress chose.

War comes first, to deliver His woe –

Then rides Pestilence wielding his bow;

Tis no use looking to God and to say 'Amen';

For here comes the third to deliver Famine.

Have you worked out who these are, before your last breath?

It's time for introductions – you've just met Death.

Your Governments have worked hard for this Memorandum –

And delivered to us an early Armageddon.

COMA

A glowing staircase before me, a fiery pit behind;
I'm stuck in between – can't make up my mind.
I glance over my shoulder down to the ground,
And see my car, wrecked, and I lay there without a sound.
Paramedics all around me, trying to revive –
They are unsure if I shall survive!
A flash of light, a whoosh in my ears, to my body I am back –
I need to communicate but unfortunately the power of speech I lack.
My body hurts – the pain immense –
What is happening? This makes no sense –
I'm now in a room with flashing lights and bleeps,
No-one can hear me speak, they think I'm asleep!
I stop trying to talk just as a Priest walks in –
He marks a cross upon my head to relieve me of sin.
The flashing lights stop, the bleeps are silenced,
I feel strange – all out of balance –
A sheet is put over my head and again I am moving,
I hear the squeak of the gurney wheels as they are turning.
Where am I now? It's cold and dark – I don't really know.
Someone has tied something to my toe.
I'm moving again – they're putting me in a coffin!
They are closing the lid…Why? Why is one of them laughing?
I'm being carried, I hear hymns, I am trying to shout;
I'm alive in here! Please let me out!
But no-one can hear and the singing then stops;

I roll forward and from behind I hear a door drop.
It's getting hot; there are flames about my head!
My last thought – I wish I were dead.

RETRIBUTION

'Come hear me now!' Said the dark voice –

I am here at your invitation, you had your choice –

'For who did you think would come,

When all your pleading was done?'

Was Heaven going to be welcoming? The Pearly Gates open wide?

Was Saint Peter going to let you inside?

What a rude awakening for you it must have been –

With all that you have preached, you seemed so clean.

But the clean was a sham, merely a veneer –

Saying the words you thought your God wanted to hear.

Well now I have heard…and I…see….you…

And now it really doesn't matter what you do.

For your race is run, along with your fun –

Your victim's father ended it with a gun;

So now and Forever with ME you reside –

With the Hounds of Hell snapping at your sides;

Do you feel the heat of my domain?

Are you feeling your victim's pain?

For what you sowed, now you shall reap –

This will not be a nice, deep sleep.

Here you stand before me, hoping I'm an illusion –

NO – I'm the FALLEN ONE – and this is RETRIBUTION.

ABANDON HOPE

I feel the dark – it calls to me, this I thought would never be;

The cold chill upon my neck, I feel your presence behind me.

The nighttime creatures in the forest abound;

Daytime friends cannot be found;

Just me and my thoughts, and my thoughts turn to you –

Your ragged cloak and scythe – everything you are, everything you do.

The darkness invokes your spirit to me,

It opens my eyes and I can see –

The darkness is not my friend – it has brought you to me;

And you are deaf to hear my plea.

For the dark is you – and you are Death –

You have come to share my last breath;

I walk with you until the ferryman's boat is near –

Alone on his ferry, I will not show fear;

I pay the ferryman his gruesome toll –

And look at the sign above the gates fixed to the wall –

The words spell out my future so very clear –

Abandon all hope all ye who enter here.

HELLBOUND

I've searched my heart and found it black –
I am Godless, a soul I lack.
All the good inside me has gone away –
A bleak emptiness is here to stay.
Save your prayers, for none can save me –
I am damned, never to be free.
I've walked through this life without remorse –
Sorrow and pain have been my life's course;
So turn your head – I don't want to be found;
My path is set – I am Hellbound.

FROM ONE LIFE TO THE NEXT

As I walk through the valley of Death, I fear nothing –
Not God, man, or breast – you won't find me grovelling;
My rod and my staff protect my life –
The rod is my strength, the staff is my wife.
They are all I need to pass this place –
Don't look for sorrow, it's not on my face.
This valley I've traversed a hundred times –
I'll not do as I'm bid, I will not sign the dotted line.
So I skip from one life to the next, I use the warrior's code –
Not Heaven or Hell will be my abode.
I leave this morbid valley to a baby's first scream –
And life and death seem just like a dream.

PAYBACK

Through my dark shroud I see your face –
This isn't the time, nor is it the place;
To right the wrongs, or heal the woes –
To forgive or forget – however that goes.
You put me here, and you are trapped by mortality –
I am now free to pay your utility;
Utility is the power for your life source –
It's now mine to play with, hear my voice.
Your deeds gave me the sanctuary of the grave –
But now I'm back…are you brave?
You need to be – because I'm here to collect my toll;
From your body I will rip out your soul –
And cast it into the pit of fire –
A little payback – I will take what I desire;
For here I stand before you – I hear you gasp –
Of me you thought you had seen your last.
Your hair turns white as you meet your host –
Goodbye old friend, I'm no forgiving Ghost.

THAT THING I DO

Here I sit at my desk, writing another ditty –
Some speak of love, some are dark; some are quite witty…
They come along out of the blue and into my head –
So instead of my book, I'm writing poems instead.
When I have written it down, I go back to the book –
After a while, I will take a look –
At the rhyme I just wrote, and sometimes I smile;
For some make me think of places I've not been in a while.
Some remind me of fears I have hidden, deep down inside –
But I type away and sometimes feel pride;
For this is what I do, and I don't really know why –
My old teachers would call it 'pie in the sky'.
But at my desk I sit each and every day –
Not really caring if it will ever pay –
And I will look over and see my wife's smiling face –
Then that's when I know I'm in my happy place.

AUTUMN

A swirling wind, and the leaves will fall –
The birds are answering their Southern call.
The quickening chill heralds the dark side of the year –
The shortening days and hazy fog are here.
Samhain is near, and we shall feast and rest -
A new year will begin with the crops from the harvest.
Tucked away indoors, the animals are safe –
Everything is in its rightful place.
Autumn's beautiful carpet of golden leaf –
Will lay on the ground, and this is my belief –
For what buds in Spring shall die in Winter,
But then burst into life again and again with splendour!
They live once more as the season demands –
Our existence in the Goddess and God's hands.
Seek your wisdom, but hurt nothing in return –
Good be your spell and long may your candle burn –
Be a part of nature, keep within its tune –
And try to live by the Witch's Rune.

THE END

A chilling mist lay over the garden of stone –
The fear inside you cuts to the bone.
For it draws close – the chase ends here –
The Beast that follows knows your fear.
Through the dark mist you see a light –
Your breath is short, your chest is tight;
But do not look back – for He draws near –
His hooded cloak, pale horse – his mindset so clear.
He wants you to feel his sharp blade,
As the sweat on your brow begins to cascade –
You trip over a small headstone,
You're looking all around – but you are quite alone.
You look up and his bony finger points, his scythe held high –
You scream out, "I don't want to die!"
But die you must, for your number is up –
You have taken a drink from the mortal Cup –
You close your eyes and witness your past deeds –
Then you are dead. You have no more needs.

HUNTER AT SIXTEEN

I sometimes think and wonder why
My son has that faraway look in his eye.
I know he can hear me but my words don't sink in –
He must have a brain, somewhere within!
Spending all day long on his PS3 –
There is no other place he would rather be!
I think he's in mourning, for his trousers hang at half-mast,
He thinks it's great…I hope it won't last!
For like all of his friends, he thinks he looks cool!
Such a shame they don't realize, they all look like fools!
His bedroom is another way of life…
In the short time he's not sleeping, it must cause him strife –
Nothing seems to phase him – he acts like a burke;
Unless the unmentionable is uttered, "Go do some work!"
Then the door slams, the moaning starts and he acts like a yob –
But he soon returns to his quivering state when you mention, "Get a job!"
Hey! Harry Enfield! Your character is reborn!
He is alive and well, and living in Thorne. :D

HOPE

I sit alone surrounded by trees;

The moonlight shines, I feel a breeze.

In the nearby grass, a circle I craft –

With the narrow end of my enchanted staff.

I draw around a veil and place my Watchtowers –

Then marvel at Nature's pure, raw powers…

The power to heal, the power to grow,

Candles to burn – candles to glow.

Wise hope for a new future to bring;

A future of light where the birds can sing!

Where children can play, and none will forbode,

Where we all can live in a safe abode.

Wouldn't that be wonderful for us all to see?

I pray for it to happen – So Mote It Be.

ANGUISH

Beverly's Autumn Skye turns 19 today –
A whole lifetime since she was taken away.
Of her short time with Bev, I've known so well –
The ones who took her will burn in Hell.
For she was 3 when they took her away,
I hear Bev talk about her every single day.
Her memory never fading, Bev looks forward with hope –
That again she will see her, if her heart can cope…
With that wonderful day when once again she will see
Her eldest baby has crossed the sea –
And knocked on her door and introduced herself, so
That Bev's heart can heal, forever more.

SIMILARITIES

As I watch my wife struggle to battle the booze –
I know it is a fight she must not lose.
Fighting battles to her is no stranger –
She knows the cost, can analyse the danger.
That amber nectar she loved to drink
Has lost its appeal and left her on the brink –
Her struggle each day reminds me of my own,
Through a dark time when bad seeds were sown.
The endless drink, night, and day –
Waiting for life to ebb away...
Night after night alone in my room –
One more drink to the oncoming gloom...
Alone amongst thousands of people –
Thinking of climbing a very high steeple.
But in my darkness a chink of light appeared –
Maybe life was not to be feared!
So I started again, and now from the drank I am free –
And for my Beverly I want this to be –
The same for her as it was for me,
To open her eyes so again she can see –
The Demon drink taken from her hand,
And to live again in her Gothic land.

DEPRESSION

The darkest of nights, the shortness of the day
Bring home the starkness in the cruellest way –
Bound by winter's dull afternoon light,
Fighting this endless bloody fight
Leaves you on the canvas, punch-drunk and sore –
There is no happiness anymore…
The days grow shorter, the nighttime bleak –
The whispered words I hear you speak;
Talk of nothingness, the Living Hell –
You are not on your own, I am there as well;
But that is okay, for I've been here before –
I've read the sign that hangs o'er the door…
What is it, my dear, that you seek?
This arduous struggle has left you weak…
Come inside and rest awhile –
STOP! TURN AROUND NOW GIRL! RUN A MILE!
Back to THIS consciousness, away from that place!
Search for the Sun to light up your face!
For once inside it is hard to leave…
No matter how hard you may plead –
That place is Solitude, Longing and Despair –
Alone in the Darkness with no-one to care…
Once that place has been visited, never do the regression –
Is that place Hell? No, it is Depression.

YULE

Yule is upon us! Oh, what a happy time –
Wonderful things for yours and mine!
But it's deeper than presents, turkey and stuffing –
It's a way we should be thinking, seeing and doing…
We must think of our actions upon this land –
See all the other people lending a hand;
And we should be doing our best to uphold
The deeds of our Forefathers, the wisdom of the old.
So when inside you bring your holly from the wood –
Work your magic truly and always for the good;
And then as a Crone, you can look back and say,
I was good to Mother Earth and I lived the Wiccan way. <3

MY TIMEPIECE

I sit on the rooftops and watch the masses pass –
I stand in the shadows with my hourglass –
Your time is mine as the sand passes through;
The sand in my timepiece flows fast and true.
From the cradle to the grave – it begins, it ends;
There is no care for your life's trends…
Whether you were good or bad,
If your life was happy or sad –
It starts when the first grain hits the bottom of the glass;
It ends when through the neck the last grain has passed.
So when you see me with hooded cloak and scythe –
Worry no more, for you've already died.

ART

I used to be an artist with paint, palette and brush –
It was all I ever wanted, and I was in a rush!
To be the next Van Gogh, my work for all to see –
To live on the banks of the Seine – Yes! That would be me!
Such was the dream of the teenage boy –
Of course, setting myself up for life to destroy;
The dream was shot down with critical aim –
It wasn't my art, but my spelling to blame!
And as a young boy I was then left in dread –
I was angry as hell now that my dream was dead!
But forty years on oh much wiser am I –
Maybe I still should have given a try;
But that is ok, I can still paint – portraits, landscapes and birds;
But instead of paints, brushes and palettes I use words!
Wouldn't that be a mindfuck to those who turned me down?
As things turned out, they didn't really make me frown –
For now with my words I paint the scenery –
Of my next book – Oh! The Irony!

THE FIGHT GOES ON

As she turns in to week number five,
All her senses are now alive!
The clouds that blocked the warming sun
Have been blown away! They are on the run!
The drink that drove her waking thoughts
Is now banished, as she has a new course –
And now a smile to lighten my day;
The drinking one has one away –
Bevie has returned! And Wednesday lives again!
The woman she was, way back when –
And to all her friends she says out loud,
That she is back! And I'm so proud –
Of how she fights, and fights again –
So much heartache, so much pain…
But that smile is now there for all to see –
Today I am so glad just to be me.

STOP THIS!

As a boy I saw man walk on the moon –
The Americans had computers that fit in a room!
We had a T.V. – it was black and white,
With a 12 inch screen – colour not yet in sight.
I played with my dog in the fields, and I was safe –
In my own little world, my own little place.
My bedroom was bare – just a bed, and a cupboard –
Whenever I was sent there, I was bored.
But look how times changed in my 50 years!
Not all of it good – some things reduce me to tears.
How knowledge has been lost – like, we need trees to breathe –
While other people starve – food, people now leave –
That the planet is warming – Governments won't listen –
To the cries of the few…the point, they are missing –
And the air that we breathe grows more and more stale,
The complexion of humans grows more and more pale.
So we walked on the moon and saw our fragile Earth in space –
And then returned to begin the destruction of the place.
My fields of play are now houses and factories –
To our leaders, this is 'progress', and quite satisfactory.
I always thought progress was to move forward –
But I really do think we are ruled by the backward –
Because if I was in power and we needed fresh air to breathe,
I certainly would not be cutting down trees!
The Earth is screaming! Why can't they hear?
They think it is theirs…and they have no fear…

Of what nature can do – they have forgotten their history;
The dinosaurs ruled, but death was their destiny.
The Earth rules ALL – keep that in mind –
You heartless Governments – when you destroy Mankind!
Then we will be gone and Earth's worst era will end –
Please try to stop the fools, my endangered friends. ☐

WHY JUDGE?

Can you see me? Or, am I invisible to you?
Do you see behind my eyes, or will you just look through?
Would you think there was something more than what you see?
Or do you have my number, and I'm all I can be…
Won't you look a little closer, spend a little more time –
I may be more than a few letters and just another rhyme;
I may be shy – a nervous nobody –
But I might be outgoing – an intelligent somebody!
You can't see past my dull clothes and timeworn face;
I may have been an Astronaut and walked in space!
But how would you know if you have made up your mind…
Your reluctance to find out is really unkind!
Please don't assume you know what I am…
I simply don't fit into your type of clan!
My dress code you would not understand…
For I don't need the latest fashion always on hand –
But clothes 'make the man' – or so your mentors say –
My clothes keep me warm on the coldest of days;
So many people judge you on what you wear –
Why is it so important to them, why do they care?
Because, ignorance abounds in a loud gathered voice –
And in this day and age, IGNORANCE is a CHOICE.

SPRINGTIME

As I wander through the forest I look up at the trees –
I admire their movements in the Springtime breeze.
To stop and take in green life starting anew –
Soon will grow bells – delicate, and blue!
The birds are singing as they line their nests –
A special place for their eggs to rest.
A busy little Dormouse scurries by –
A female mouse has caught his eye!
Blessings from nature as the sap begins to rise –
The delicate mist and a new sunrise.
The Robin sings her sweet enchanting song –
She is pleased that the Winter has gone;
The squirrels scamper from tree to tree –
All of Pan's animals are quick, and free –
The ladybird warms her back in the morning sun;
Springtime really has begun.
All thoughts of the Winter cold now have to wane,
As we draw closer to Beltane.

WOE IS ME

It's so easy to feel sorry for oneself and proclaim, 'Woe is me'…
But does it help in any way, or do your woes still be?
I very seldom talk of woe, although I've known it well –
I like to be a happy sort, I think that you can tell.
Sometimes I see tragedy, but that word is overused –
For some people's tragedies cause others to be amused.
An animal killed or a tree chopped down is a tragedy to me –
But to some, their football team losing is a tragedy.
Young people living rough and poverty should be our leaders woe –
But party on they do, and are happy to let that go –
I have always used the thought there are people worse than me,
And this has helped me live my life with much less misery.
There truly are some folks who really have it bad –
And my heart goes out to all of them it makes me feel quite sad.
But many of us complain too much, not realizing we are blessed –
With love, and food, and happiness – even how we are dressed!
So the next time the shroud of Woe seems to cover you,
Try to count your blessings, it just might pull you through.

HELP THE BEES (A POEM FOR MORGANA)

To eat the apples from the trees,

They must be pollinated by the bees!

For all of us who understand –

Know the bees do need a hand.

Grow some flowers for them to find –

Show the Earth that you are kind.

Our bees provide all that we need;

From everything that grows from seed.

John Paul Bernett

I hope you enjoyed these little ditties…I had fun writing them – and there are lots more where they came from! For more information on my writing (novels and poetry), please visit my Facebook page at: https://www.facebook.com/JpBernettAuthor

If you like the page, please click my 'like' button! Thank you very much for reading   ☐ <3